pete the puppy

by Gisela Buck and Siegfried Buck

For a free color catalog describing Gareth Stevens' list of high-quality books, call 1-800-542-2595 (USA) or 1-800-461-9120 (Canada). Gareth Stevens' Fax: (414) 225-0377.

Library of Congress Cataloging-in-Publication Data available upon request from publisher. Fax: (414) 225-0377 for the attention of the Publishing Records Department.

ISBN 0-8368-1501-7

This North American edition first published in 1996 by
Gareth Stevens Publishing
1555 North RiverCenter Drive, Suite 201
Milwaukee, Wisconsin 53212 USA

This edition first published in 1996 by Gareth Stevens, Inc. Original edition © 1994 by Kinderbuchverlag KBV Luzern (Sauerländer, AG), Aarau, Switzerland, under the title *Kasimir, das Dackelkind*. Translated from the German by John E. Hayes. Adapted by Gareth Stevens, Inc. All additional material supplied for this edition © 1996 by Gareth Stevens, Inc.

Photographer: Andreas Fischer-Nagel
Watercolor artist: Wolfgang Kill
Series editor: Patricia Lantier-Sampon
Editorial assistants: Diane Laska, Jamie Daniel

Printed in Mexico
1 2 3 4 5 6 7 8 9 9 99 98 97 96

Gareth Stevens Publishing
MILWAUKEE

Pete's mother has given birth to four puppies.

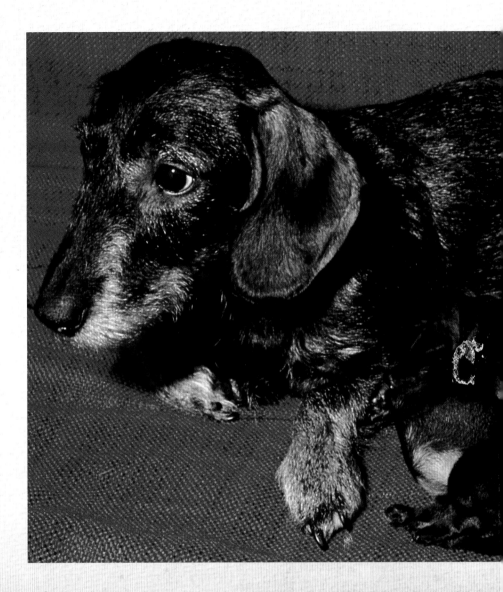

All the puppies in this litter have names starting with the same letter — *p*. From the left, they are Perry, Penny, Pal, and Pete.

3

Perry, Penny, Pal, and Pete lie
close together. They feel safe
like this.

After ten days, Pete opens his eyes.
It takes a few days, however, before
he can see clearly.

After about two weeks, Pete
can smell the world around
him. After three weeks, he
can hear, too.

Pete begins to explore his basket. This is hard work. Every now and then, he plops down for a rest!

For the first time, Perry, Penny, Pal, and Pete go outdoors. Pete sniffs excitedly around in the grass.

Pete sees, hears, and smells
many new things in the grass.
He's just a little confused.

9

Food is set out in bowls in the yard.

Pete and Penny think it tastes good.

Pal prefers to drink milk, or nurse,

from his mother.

The puppies play a fun
game with the bowls.
Pete doesn't want to
give up his bowl.

What is Pete whispering
in Penny's ear? Maybe
he is asking: "Should we
go on an expedition?"

They bravely march off together.

Pete carefully crosses a stream.

Penny follows him.

They get very thirsty.

The water tastes great!

Pete finds a piece of wood.

He gnaws and chews on it.

It crunches like a bone.

Chewing up wood is fun!
But play-fighting with Penny
is fun, too.

The puppies don't really fight. They
get along just fine together.

They find a real meat bone!
Now they can tear at the meat
together. The bone is too thick
and hard for them to chew up.

After about eight weeks, Pete is
vaccinated against dangerous diseases.

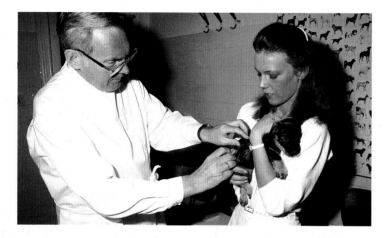

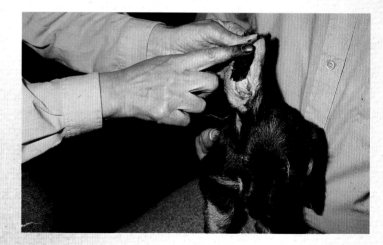

Pete is a pure breed.
In this case, a number
is inked into his ear.

This number is entered
in his pedigree album.

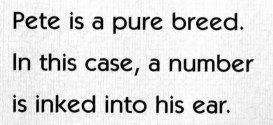

Pete is independent now. He can run around on his own. Lisa's grandmother bought him.

Pete and Lisa are becoming good friends.

Pete is growing quickly.
He wants to play with Lisa's
little tiger cat, but the cat is
afraid of him.

Lisa's orange cat is not afraid.
Pete makes friends with her.

One day, Pete comes across a strange animal in the yard.

Pete goes right up to the animal. The hedgehog's spines prick him on the nose!

Pete will be more careful next time.

Pete is learning how to walk on a leash.
He will be a good hunting dog one day.

Lisa's grandmother and her other
dachshund, Asta, show Pete what a
hunting dog must be able to do.
Pete gets excited when they take a
walk in the forest. He will learn quickly.

Further Reading and Videos

A First Look at Dogs. Selsam and Hunt (Walker)
Animal Stories. (Atlas Video)
Animals At A Glance (4 volumes). (Gareth Stevens)
Baby Animals: Puppies. Kate Petty (Barron)
How Puppies Grow. Millicent E. Selsam (Scholastic)
I Can Read About Dogs and Puppies. J. I. Anderson (Troll)
Man's Best Friend. (PBS Nature Series Video)
Only One Woof. James Herriot (St. Martin)
Pet Show. (LCA Video)
The Three Pups. M. Porter and A. Aymerich (Hampton-Brown)
Your First Puppy. Marcel Carpentier (TFH Publishers)

Fun Facts about Puppies and Dogs

Did you know . . .

— that all the types of dogs kept as pets are relatives of wolves?

— that a puppy with parent dogs that are from two different pure breeds is called a "mix"?

— that a puppy with parents that are themselves mixes of many different breeds is called a "mutt"?

— that some puppies are specially trained to be guide dogs to help people who can't see or hear?

— that puppies grow teeth, just like human babies, and because of this need things to chew on to help their teeth come in?

Glossary-Index

breed — a particular type or variety of animal (pp. 18, 23).

confused — puzzled; not able to understand something (p. 9).

expedition — a trip that is taken for a specific purpose (p. 12).

gnaw — to chew on for a long time (p. 14).

hedgehogs — small animals that live in Europe and have sharp spines on their backs (p. 21).

independent — capable of living on one's own (p. 19).

leash — a chain or strap attached to a collar and used to hold or lead an animal from place to place (p. 22).

litter — a number of animals that are born together from one mother (p. 3).

nurse — to drink the milk produced by a female mammal's body; puppies nurse for several weeks before they can eat any other kind of food (p. 10).

pedigree album — a book that lists the records of a purebred dog's pedigree, or list of ancestors, as proof that he or she is purebred (p. 18).

pure breeds — animals that are produced by parents that are from many generations of the same breed (p. 18).

vaccinate — to give an animal or human a shot as protection against certain diseases (p. 18).